Pat and Bob;

With our best wishes and hoping that our friendship will continue.

Müminuvel and Naif Ataly

Lefkoşe, Kıbrıs   26 May 1988

HIGH ABOVE
KIBRIS

Copyright © 1987 Three's Company

All rights reserved. No part of this publication may be reproduced or transmitted in any form or by any means, electronic or mechanical, including photocopy, recording, or any information storage and retrieval system, without permission in writing from the publisher.

First published in Kıbrıs

ISBN 0 9512766 0 3

Designed and produced by Three's Company 12 Flitcroft Street London WC2H 8DJ Great Britain

Photographs © 1987 Sonia Halliday and Laura Lushington

Co-edition organized and produced by Angus Hudson Ltd Greater London House Hampstead Road London NW1 7QX Great Britain

Design: Peter Wyart MSIAD

Typesetting by Watermark Hampermill Cottage, Watford, Hertfordshire

Printed in Great Britain by Purnell Book Production Ltd Paulton, Bristol

Foreword

I have no doubt that this superb book will inspire and inform all those who want to become better acquainted with Kıbrıs, the Turkish Republic of Northern Cyprus.

The photographs contained in this book give some idea of the striking beauty of Northern Cyprus, and help to unfold its unique history. The peace and tranquillity of our young state is clearly reflected in the beautiful photographs so expertly taken by the talented photographers, Sonia Halliday and Laura Lushington, to whose enterprising spirit and devotion we owe this book.

The natural beauty and fascinating history of our land is matched by the warm hospitality of the Turkish Cypriot people, who are gallantly striving together to build up their new nation. I am happy to say that, almost without exception, every newcomer to Northern Cyprus becomes a regular visitor! I am sure that this beautiful book will attract many new friends to our country, and that our 'old friends' — our regular visitors — will find it a gift to treasure at home.

Enjoy this book, and come back to us with your friends. You owe yourself a good holiday, and the Turkish Republic of Northern Cyprus eagerly awaits you.

Rauf R. Denktaş
President of the Turkish Republic of Northern Cyprus

The Turkish Republic of Northern Cyprus

HIGH ABOVE KIBRIS

UNIQUE AERIAL PHOTOGRAPHS
BY SONIA HALLIDAY AND LAURA LUSHINGTON
TEXT BY TIM DOWLEY

KIBRIS

The Turkish Republic of Northern Cyprus

MEDITERRANEAN SEA

Zafer Burnu

KARPAZ

Kumyali

GIRNE RANGE

Kantara Castle

Bogaz

Esentepe

Beş Parmak Daği

Buffavento Castle

Bellapais Abbey

GIRNE
(Kyrenia)

Karaman

St Hilarion Castle

Karşıyaka

GÜZELYURT

Vuni

Lefka

Erenköy

MESARYA

Geçitkale Airport

Salamis

Tuzla

GAZI MAGOSA
(Famagusta)

LEFKOSA
(Nicosia)

Ercan Airport

N

Scale

0   5   10   15   20   25 kilometres

0   5   10   15   miles

Major Road

CONTENTS

Introduction

Strategically sited in the middle of the eastern Mediterranean, astride some of the most ancient trading routes in the world, the history of the island of Cyprus reads like a roll-call of lost empires. Cyprus straddled the great routeways from the Hittite Empire in Anatolia to Egypt; from Mesopotamia to the Aegean; from Phoenicia to the West; from the Italian city-states of Venice and Genoa to the East; and, in more recent times, from Britain to India through the Suez Canal.

Several main periods may be clearly identified in the history of Cyprus, and each is reflected in the historical monuments that the visitor can see today.

Even in the earliest period of human development, the Stone Age, there is evidence in Cyprus of trading contacts across the sea. Archaeologists have discovered stone-cutting tools sharpened with obsidian, a rock which does not occur naturally on the island. But it was the beginning of the Bronze Age, about 2300 B.C., that first gave Cyprus its role as a commercial centre in the eastern Mediterranean.

A shepherd on his mule near Beş Parmak Dağı (Pentadactylos – Five Finger Mountain)

Scholars still argue over which came first — the name of the island or the name of the copper found in it. But whatever the answer to that question, there is no doubt that it was Cypriot copper, together with tin from Sinai, and later from Spain and Cornwall, England, which provided the basis of the Bronze Age in this area. Cyprus became a major exporter of both copper and timber. Though bronze gave way to iron about 1050 B.C., and the importance of Cyprus consequently diminished, the island's geographical position ensured its continuing role.

Merchants from Greece, the Aegean islands and from Aleas who had settled in Cilicia on the southern coast of Anatolia competed with Phoenicians from the east to establish first trading posts and then settled colonies on the island. The arrival of the armies of the Persian Empire in the eastern Mediterranean about 550 B.C. brought to the little city-states of Cyprus a degree of unity that they had never achieved on their own. Under Evagoras I, king of Salamis, Cyprus came nearest to becoming a single kingdom. But after his death in 374 B.C. the island was competed for by the rival great powers of Persia and of Macedonia under Alexander the Great and his successors, Antigonus and Ptolemy. A further period of political confusion followed, only brought to an end in 58 B.C. with the annexation of the whole island by Rome. The Romans established Cyprus as a proconsular province within the Roman Empire and transferred the administrative capital from Salamis to Paphos.

Under the Pax Romana, and particularly after the Roman general Pompey had defeated the Cilician pirates, Cyprus developed its great potential as foremost trading centre of the eastern empire. Its importance is reflected in the splendid ruins of Roman Salamis, with its extensive public works such as harbours, roads and aqueducts. In A.D. 45 St Paul visited Salamis with his companion, the Cyprus-born St Barnabas, and Sergius Paulus, the Governor of Paphos, was converted to Christianity.

In A.D. 330, Cyprus became part of the Byzantine Empire of Constantine the Great. Unfortunately the island lies in a seismic zone, and in A.D. 332 and 342 the city of Salamis was almost wholly destroyed by earthquakes. The city was rebuilt by the Byzantines and renamed Constantia, only to come under threat from the emergent Islamic Arab powers in Damascus and Baghdad. Arab raids were finally ended by the Emperor Phocas in the mid-tenth century, but by then Salamis (or Constantia) had been abandoned to the sand-dunes.

After a brief interlude of unified, but despotic, rule under the self-styled emperor Isaac Comnenus in the late twelfth century, Cyprus forged new links with the West as a staging post on the way to the Crusades. King Richard I

A traditional folklore dance team at Girne (Kyrenia) Castle.

of England, 'The Lionheart', celebrated his marriage to the Princess Berengaria of Navarre in Limassol in 1191, and then defeated Isaac Comnenus in battle. Richard continued on his way to the Holy Land, but, finding that money for the crusade was running out, sold his rights to the Kingdom of Cyprus to the Christian order of the Knights Templar. When they, in turn, found the burden of ruling Cyprus too great, they handed Cyprus back to Richard.

By good fortune there was in Richard's retinue ex-king Guy de Lusignan, who had been deposed from his throne as King of Jerusalem by the Saracens. Richard offered Guy the crown of Cyprus, which he accepted, thereby initiating almost three hundred years of feudal rule by the Lusignan dynasty, which gave Cyprus a welcome breathing-space from internal and external strife, and resulted in a brilliant flowering of medieval art and architecture, much of which can still be seen in the royal castles and in the abbey of Bellapais. During the Lusignan period, the activities of the Orthodox church were strictly forbidden.

After the fall of the port of Acre in Palestine to the Saracens in 1291, Gazi Magosa (Famagusta) inherited the proud position of chief eastern Mediterranean entrepot for trade from the East with Europe. Travellers from the West marvelled at the wealth of the merchants of Gazi Magosa (Famagusta), and at the huge walls built for its defence.

However the Lusignans were losing control over the island, and first the Genoese and then the Venetians took over. The Venetians ruled Cyprus from 1489 until 1571, strengthening the fortifications of Lefkoşa (Nicosia) and Gazi Magosa (Famagusta), but doing little for the native population.

When in 1570 a great Turkish force arrived to besiege Gazi Magosa (Famagusta), the city held out for ten months before finally being forced to surrender. The walled cities of Lefkoşa (Nicosia) and Girne (Kyrenia) had already surrendered to their besieging forces, so that in 1571 the Ottoman Turks took control of the entire island.

Within the vast Ottoman Empire, the island of Cyprus was only a small province, whose main preoccupation was to ensure that the prescribed annual tribute was duly paid to Istanbul. Even so, the Cypriots were given a large measure of autonomy by their Turkish masters. The Greek Orthodox church was given supremacy over all other Christian churches on the island, and its archbishop recognized as the political head of the community. Economic development was, however, slow, and little capital investment was forthcoming.

In 1878 Turkey leased the island to Great Britain, which became responsible for administration and defence, although the Sultan retained ultimate authority. This opened up new prospects of development and economic expansion. Harbours and roads, schools and hospitals were built, while the local administration was reorganized on the lines of other British colonial dependencies. In 1925, Cyprus became a British Crown Colony.

Cyprus was declared a republic on 16 August 1960, while remaining a member of the British Commonwealth. Independence was granted on the basis of a partnership in government between the Greek and Turkish Cypriot communities, with the government made up of seventy per cent Greeks and thirty per cent Turks. However, as a result of a coup d'état in December 1963, the Greek Cypriots controlled the government of the island for the next eleven years.

Finally in 1975 the Turkish Cypriot people set up their own independent state in Northern Cyprus, Kıbrıs, to match the Greek Cypriot state in Southern Cyprus. Although the UN Secretary General has made repeated efforts to bring about an agreed settlement between the two communities, as yet this has been without success.

Photographing Kıbrıs

We have both known and loved Kıbrıs for many years. The idea of photographing it from the air grew out of our larger plan to create a comprehensive book of aerial photographs of sites of biblical interest. We used a Cessna with the door removed, flown by two able and experienced pilots sympathetic to the needs of aerial photography. We photographed mainly at heights between 100 and 500 feet above our subjects, using two 6×7cm Pentax cameras, and two 35mm Pentax LX cameras with 70–210mm zoom lenses. The cameras were all strung on a fine safety cable locked around our waists and the seats, as there is a real danger of hanging yourself if the cameras are wound around your neck!

This aerial project was an amazing feat for Laura, since her right hand was in an 'abduction' splint, following a serious car accident in England, when an articulated lorry jack-knifed into our car, smashing her shoulder. Laura's camera was fitted with a pistol grip and automatic wind-on, enabling her to shoot left-handed.

To other photographers' surprise, we used comparatively slow film, Ektachrome Professional EPN 120 (100 ASA), since 400 ASA film tends to give a blue cast, especially in aerial photography. We found that with 100 ASA film the colour reproduction was excellent, shooting at 1/1000 second at f/4 or f/5.6, depending on the colour density of the land below. We used 135mm and 105mm lenses, except for the theatre and basilica at Salamis, where we used the 300mm lens to obtain close-ups.

From the air, we not only saw the ancient sites from a new vantage point, but the forests and escarpments took on fresh dimensions. It also became clear to us that the archaeological sites of Northern Cyprus remain largely unexplored; given sufficient financial support, archaeologists could undoubtedly discover much more about the role of this unique island in the history of the eastern Mediterranean.

In photographing for this book, we made a total of three flights. The first day's flying was very bumpy, and after just an hour circling Salamis and then Kantara Castle we called it a day because as soon as we had satisfactorily lined up our subject the plane hit an air-pocket!

The second day the weather was perfect. We flew in low over ancient Salamis. Since it was November, and the giant

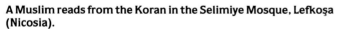

A Muslim reads from the Koran in the Selimiye Mosque, Lefkoşa (Nicosia).

The photographers, Laura Lushington (left) and Sonia Halliday (right) with Hilmi Özen, Director of the State Theatre of Kıbrıs (Northern Cyprus), at Girne (Kyrenia) Harbour.

yellow fennel which is so profuse in spring had been burnt off in the summer heat, we had a clear view of the ruins of the Roman city. Flying from Salamis to Gazi Magosa (Famagusta) took only a few minutes. The city is immediately recognizable by the ancient wall surrounding the old city, and by the prominent Lâla Mustafa Paşa Mosque, dating from the fourteenth century.

Having finished photographing over Gazi Magosa (Famagusta) we flew north along the coast to Kantara Castle, from which we could see the Karpas (Kirpasa) Peninsula stretching away to the east. In spring the Karpas (Kirpasa) is a botanist's paradise, with literally hundreds of different species of wild flowers. We plan to publish a book devoted entirely to the wild flowers of Kıbrıs.

We then flew along the Girne (Kyrenia) Range, passing over Beş Parmak Dağı (Pentadactylos – Five Finger Mountain), and Buffavento and St Hilarion Castles. Since all three castles are built atop the highest peaks in the range, it is only possible to photograph the walls and towers from the air. Similarly, we were able to photograph head-on the north façade of Bellapais Abbey, which nestles in the foothills below Buffavento, a view inaccessible to the photographer on the ground.

We next flew at 100 feet over the town of Girne (Kyrenia), so that the massive castle walls more than filled our lenses. Then, gaining height, we obtained some longer shots of Girne (Kyrenia) from above the little village of Karaman (Karmi), before flying through the Bogaz Pass to Lefkoşa (Nicosia).

On the third day we flew across the Mesarya (Mesaoria) Plain, with its characteristic dry river beds, to the citrus groves around Güzelyurt (Morphou), so vital to the economy of Kıbrıs (Northern Cyprus), then out over the deep blue sea before circling back over the promontory where the ruins of the palace of Vuni (Vouni) stand. From this point, the southern coast of Turkey can be seen on a clear day. Our final objective was Tuzla (Engomi-Alasia), back at the eastern end of the Mesarya (Mesaoria) Plain.

Sonia Halliday and Laura Lushington, May 1987

Lefkoşa (Nicosia)

Lefkoşa (Nicosia) stands in the middle of the Plain of Mesarya (Mesaoria), and on the right bank of the River Kanlı (Pedias). A city has stood here from the Early Bronze Age (3000 B.C.) from which period a number of tombs have been discovered. The ancient city of Ledra, allegedly founded by Lefcon, son of Ptolemy Soter in 280 B.C., may have been situated here. However, the first written record of the city comes only in A.D. 1211, when Wilbrand, Count of Oldenburg in Germany, visited Cyprus during a pilgrimage to the Holy Land.

Although Lefkoşa (Nicosia) was fortified with walls and towers during the Middle Ages, the occupying Venetians replaced these with ramparts and eleven bastions in the sixteenth century, the better to defend the city with cannon. Although in recent times the town has spread outside the walls, the main commercial area is still concentrated in the old city.

Among the notable buildings of Lefkoşa (Nicosia) is the Tekke of the Mevlevi Dervishes, now a museum. The Tekke was built in the early seventeenth century and was used by Moslem sect for mystic dances until 1930.

The Selimiye Mosque, originally the Cathedral of Santa Sophia, was consecrated in 1326, and converted into a

mosque in 1570. The building suffered severe earthquake damage in 1491 and 1547. The building was one of the great Lusignan monuments of the Near East, and is now the chief mosque of northern Cyprus.

Lefkoşa also features two khans, used until recently as caravanserai. These are the Buyuk Khan (or 'big inn'), and the Kumardjilar Khan, both dating from about 1570.

In the aerial picture, the Girne (Kyrenia) Range can be seen in the distance.

Inset: The building was originally constructed by the Lusignans in 1329 as the Latin Archbishopric Palace. The Second floor was built after 1571 by the Ottomans. It was the residence of the first chief judge Menteşoğlu.

Tuzla (Engomi-Alasia) was first investigated by a British expedition in 1896, and first excavated in 1913. Archaeologists discovered that the ruins marked the site of Alasia, capital of Cyprus in the fifteenth century B.C. In the thirteenth century B.C. the Mycenaeans occupied the city, finally abandoning it in the eleventh century, following a disastrous earthquake and fire.

Alasia was superseded by the nearby city of Salamis, but after its fall it provided a burial place for the rulers of Salamis. An area of some two square miles, stretching from Yeniboğaziçi (Agios Sergios) to Tuzla (Engomi-Alasia), is honeycombed with tombs dating from this period. Many of these tombs have been excavated by archaeologists, but all except seven have been covered up again to prevent looting.

Below: Part of the remains of Tuzla (Engomi-Alasia). There is a marked similarity with Mycenaean sites elsewhere in the Mediterranean.

Salamis Bay

The ancient city of Salamis was reputedly founded by the Greek prince Teucer, son of Telamon, king of the island of Salamis, on his return from the Trojan War, about 1184 B.C. The ancient city of Salamis covered one square mile and was very prosperous, with many great public buildings. Salamis remained the principal city of Cyprus until the Romans transferred the island's capital to Paphos.

In ancient times, the town had a fine harbour, making Salamis an important trading post in the eastern Mediterranean. However, repeated earthquakes, particularly severe in A.D. 332 and 342, devastated the city and destroyed the port. Although Salamis was rebuilt by the Byzantines, and renamed Constantia, it was finally destroyed soon after A.D. 647, following its capture by the Syrian Arabs. Until the early twentieth century the entire site was buried beneath sand-dunes, but since then it has been excavated and some parts left uncovered.

The Salamis Bay Hotel, near the site of ancient Salamis.

Theatre, Salamis

Among the most impressive remains from ancient Salamis is the huge Roman theatre. The theatre was built early in the imperial period, probably during the rule of the Emperor Augustus (27 B.C. – A.D. 14), and was repaired and remodelled during the first and second centuries. The theatre could originally hold several thousand spectators in its fifty rows of tiered seats. Built to stage both plays and spectacles, the theatre declined in use during the Byzantine period, when church-going was encouraged at the expense of popular entertainment. The Byzantines also stripped the building of much of its decorative marble and its statues so that today the theatre appears notably bare.

The theatre, like much of ancient Salamis, was buried under the sand for centuries, and only re-discovered in 1959. During the last twenty-five years much effort has been devoted to restoring the theatre so that public performances can once more be staged there, utilising the fine acoustics of the original design.

The tiered seating of the theatre. The wall supporting the back seats rises to a height of 54 feet (20 metres).

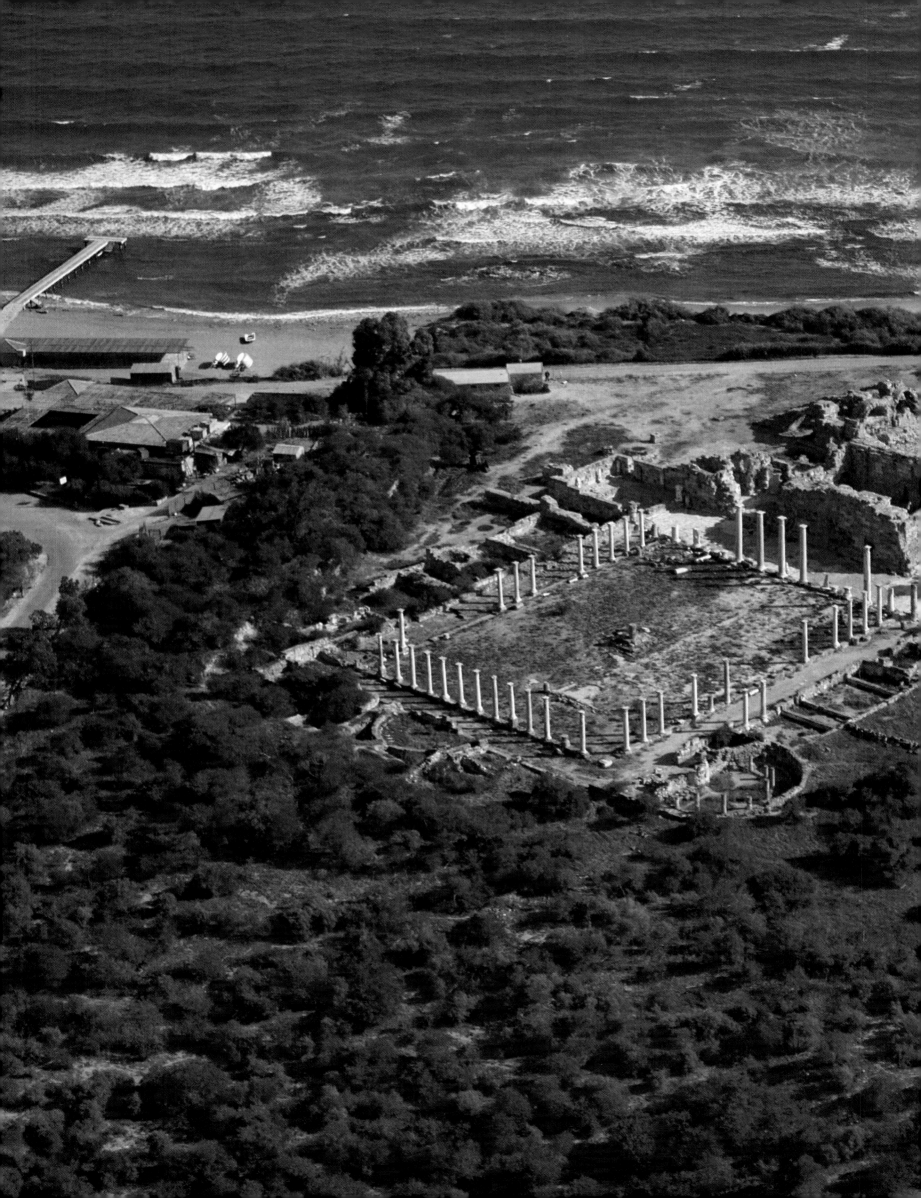

Gymnasium, Salamis

The other spectacular ruin at Salamis is that of the ancient gymnasium, with its distinctive pillars. The building, as its name suggests, was originally designed to provide a venue for citizens wishing to exercise, and was initially constructed by Ptolemy V Epiphanes during the second century B.C., while parts of it were restored and added to by the Romans between the second century B.C. and the second century A.D. Nearby stood an elaborate network of baths, where the sportsmen could relax and bathe after their gymnastic exertions.

The fifty-ton marble pillars which supported the gymnasium were brought from Turkey, Greece or Italy. Like the rest of the city, the gymnasium was badly damaged during the fourth-century earthquakes, although the Byzantines attempted to re-erect the pillars following the disaster. However the gymnasium was eventually buried beneath the sand, and only re-discovered in 1882. In 1955 the task of re-erecting the columns once more was completed, although the shafts have not always been matched with their proper capitals.

The northern annexe of the gymnasium. It has been suggested that the statues lost their heads to treasure-hunters during the European Renaissance. However during excavations at Salamis several heads were discovered buried in various parts of the site. They were probably broken off as a result of religious prohibitions, or perhaps accidentally.

Basilica of Campana Petra, Salamis

The basilica of Campana Petra, which is near the ancient harbour, is the only one of the three basilica churches at Salamis with some of its walls still standing. Built on the same pattern as the Roman law-court, or 'basilica', the building consisted of a long hall with a central nave and side aisles, and a semi-circular apse at the front. In the case of the Roman law-court, this was where the judge sat; in the case of the Christian church, it was where the bishop's throne stood. The basilica was erected some time after A.D. 400, and probably fell into disuse around A.D. 900 when Salamis was abandoned.

Salamis had Christian connections from early in the Christian era; St Paul came here around A.D. 45, at the start of his first missionary journey, accompanied by St Barnabas, a native of Cyprus. They landed at Salamis harbour, and preached in the Jewish synagogues of the Roman city (Acts 15:5).

Below: The monastery of St Barnabas, near Salamis. Named after Paul's companion. Nearby is a rock tomb, reputed to be that of St Barnabas.

Gazi Magosa
(Famagusta)

The origins of Gazi Magosa (Famagusta) are obscure. Some have claimed that the town was founded between 285 and 247 B.C. by Ptolemy Philadelphus of Egypt. Certainly by the beginning of the fourteenth century A.D. it had become a major commercial centre for the eastern Mediterranean, and the headquarters of several Christian religious orders. Growing rich during this period on the trade conducted by Genoese and Venetian merchants, massive walls were constructed around Gazi Magosa (Famagusta) to defend the city and its vital harbour.

After bitter conflict with the Genoese, the Venetians took control of the island in 1489. But Venetian rule lasted only eighty-two years; in 1570 the Turkish fleet appeared outside the town, and, after a siege lasting ten months, the Ottoman Turks captured both the city and the island.

Below: The Lâla Mustafa Paşa Mosque, Gazi Magosa (Famagusta). This was originally the cathedral of St Nicholas, constructed in the French Gothic style during the thirteenth and fourteenth centuries. The Lusignans were crowned Kings of Jerusalem in this cathedral. On taking the town, the Turks added a minaret to the cathedral and converted it into an Islamic mosque. In 1954 it was renamed the Lâla Mustafa Paşa Mosque, after the Ottoman military commander during the siege of 1570.

City Walls, Gazi Magosa (Famagusta)

It was the Lusignan rulers of Cyprus who began building the impressive fortifications which today surround the old city of Gazi Magosa (Famagusta). But with the invention of gunpowder and introduction of cannon there came major changes in military architecture. In place of high, crenellated walls, ideal for defence against bows and arrows, catapults or battering rams, there came lower, sloping walls and round towers. Gun chambers inside the defensive walls were provided with chimneys to allow the suffocating smoke from the cannon to escape. Between 1490 and 1550 the Venetians totally remodelled the walls and towers of Gazi Magosa (Famagusta) to make them defensible in the new age of the cannon. The aerial picture shows a stretch of the southern walls of the city as rebuilt by the Venetians.

Below: Othello's Tower (The Citadel). Although Shakespeare's Othello is a largely fictitious character, and the playwright mentions only 'a seaport in Cyprus', Othello's name has become inextricably linked with the citadel of Gazi Magosa (Famagusta). Over the main gateway is a marble slab bearing the winged lion of St Mark, the symbol of Venice.

Girne (Kyrenia) Range

The north coast of Cyprus is dominated by the Girne (Kyrenia) Range of mountains, a long, narrow upthrust of limestone peaks stretching from Zafer Burnu (Cape Andreas) in the east to Karşiyaka (Vasilia) in the west. Some 110 miles (175 kilometres) long, the range runs parallel to the north coast of the island, only touching the coast at three points, Kayalar (Orga), Yedikonuk (Ephtakomi) and Zafer Burnu (Cape Andreas). For the most part, the upper slopes of the mountains are forested with conifers, while the narrow coastal plain has rich alluvial soils which can support crops such as olives, carob beans, grapes and citrus fruit. South of the Girne (Kyrenia) Range lies the plain of Mesarya (Mesaoria), which means 'between the mountains'. The aerial picture looks west along the range.

Inset: A shepherd boy with his flock in the northern foothills of the Girne (Kyrenia) Range, near Esentepe (Ayios Amvrosios).

Kantara Castle

The Girne (Kyrenia) Range of mountains provided a fine natural defence against invaders from the sea. From early times fortresses were built in these mountains to take advantage of the natural defences. The ruins of three major strongholds still survive: Kantara in the east, Buffavento in the central area, and St Hilarion towards the west. The castle of Kantara first appears in the records in 1191, when the self-styled King Isaac Comnenus of Cyprus took refuge here from Richard the Lionheart of England.

Kantara Castle guards both the north coast of Cyprus and the entrance to the Karpas (Kirpasa) peninsula to the east. Built at a height of 2068 feet (630 metres) it stands on an isolated mass of rock, with a steep drop on three sides and a fortified gateway on the east. Although the Venetians abandoned the castle in the mid-sixteenth century, parts of the building are well-preserved, with a number of the vaulted chambers still retaining their roofs. The ruins were strengthened and made safe in 1914.

Below: The north-east tower and wall, Kantara Castle.

Beş Parmak Dağı
(Pentadactylos – Five Finger Mountain)

This distinctively-shaped mountain, its five peaks resembling the fingers of the hand (hence the Turkish and Greek names), has lent its name to the entire Girne (Kyrenia) Range, although modern mapmakers ignore this local tradition. The mountain lies some ten miles (sixteen kilometres) east of Girne (Kyrenia), overlooking the main road to Gazi Magosa (Famagusta). The 'fingers' are most clearly seen from the south or from Lefkoşa (Nicosia); from the north the resemblance is not nearly so marked.

The mountain consists of a limestone ridge, detached from, but parallel to, the main Girne (Kyrenia) Range. Its highest peak, the 'middle finger', reaches 2429 feet (741 metres), but is far from being the highest in the range. The 'fingers' of the mountain were probably originally formed by faulting in the limestone rock, which has subsequently been weathered away by solution in rainwater.

Inset: Goats among the rocks and pines below Beş Parmak Dağı (Pentadactylos – Five Finger Mountain).

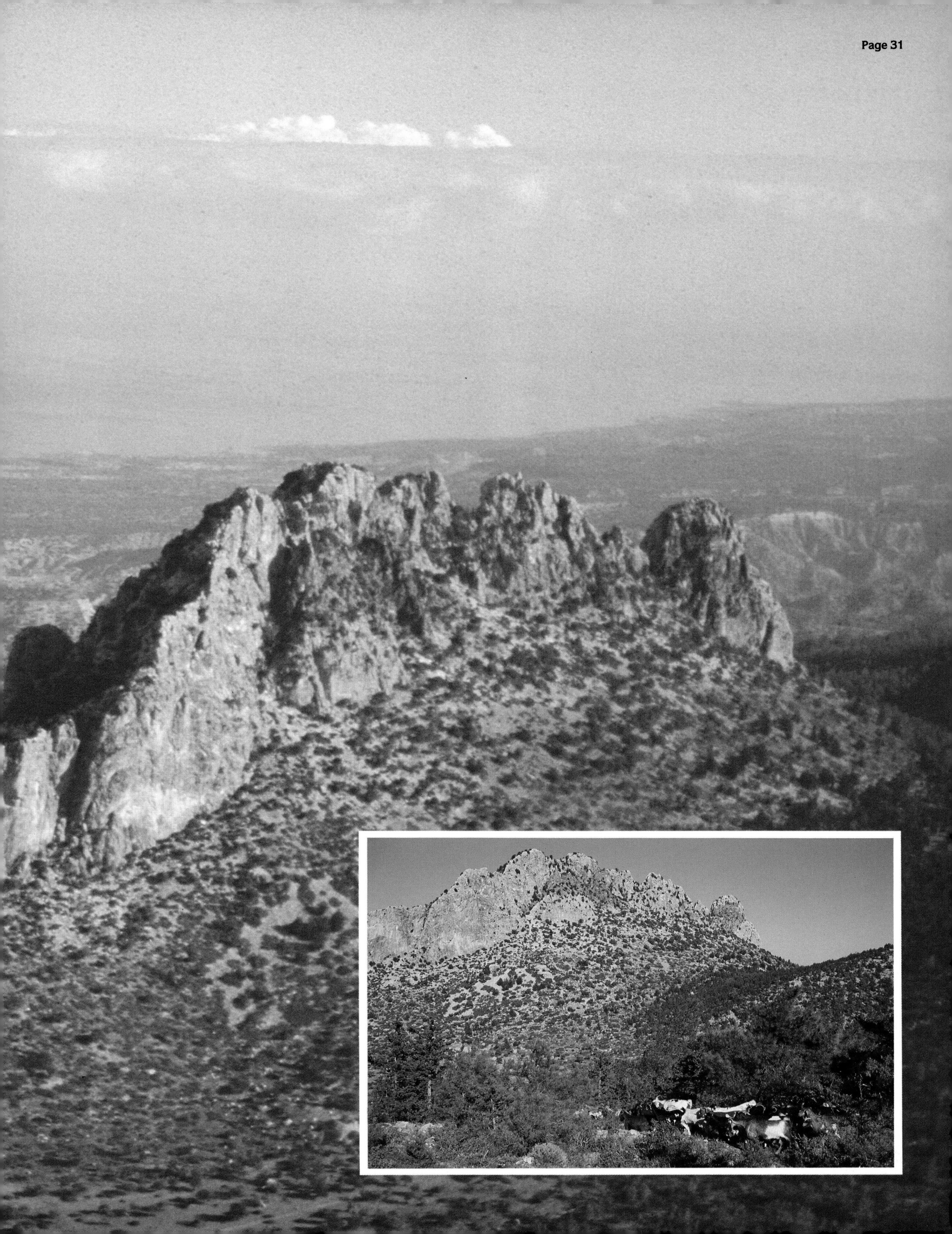

Wild Flowers of Kıbrıs

Kıbrıs – and particularly the Karpas (Kirpasa) peninsula – is a botanist's paradise, with literally hundreds of species of wild flowers. For instance the foothills of the Girne (Kyrenia) Range are carpeted with the yellow *Ranunculus asiaticus*, a member of the buttercup family, though often mistaken for the anemone. (The easiest way to differentiate between the two is by the fact that the anemone has a 'bract' or leaf-like structure around its stem below the petals.)

The *Ranunculus asiaticus* can be found in several colours – yellow, flushed with red, white/cream, and carmine and plain white. A completely carmine specimen is very rare. The *Ranunculus* varies in size from 2 – 5 centimetres across and 6 – 18 centimetres high.

The anemone is found in the olive groves and the foothills until the beginning of April, although the main season is finished by the end of March. The red crown anemone is becoming rarer; in 1955 the present writers saw it in the middle ward of St Hilarion Castle; today it is only found rarely in cornfields. The tulip has a fairly short season (March only), and grows in the cornfields near Gecitkale, Camlibel and Tebebasi, all in the north-east. The tulips are often difficult to spot, since they are shorter than the corn. The *Gladiolus segetum* (which means cornfield in Latin; it too grows in cornfields) is easier to see since it grows taller.

Often there is a complete field or olive grove of yellow, which can be the crown daisy or the oxalis, sometimes interspersed with blue, either anchusa or the tassel hyacinth (*Muscari comosum*). The Red Horned poppy is fairly rare; the present writers only found it growing on the roadside near Kantara. The pink and white rock-roses (*Cistus*) make a beautiful showing on many of the mountainsides as well as on rocky terrain a few metres above sea level. The miniature asphodel is very rare indeed.

The cyclamen grows in profusion everywhere along the roadside and in every cranny on the mountainside. The miniature blue iris (*Sisyrinchium*), often as small as 6 centimetres in height, grows to within a few metres of the sea, while on the plain and in the mountains it can reach a height of 30 centimetres.

Sonia Halliday and Laura Lushington

Tulip (*Tulipa praecox*)

Purple viper's bugloss (*Echium lycopsis*)

Green-winged orchid (*Orchis morio*)

Tongue orchid (*Serapias vomeracea*)

Crown anemone (*Anemone coronaria*)

Wild hyacinth (*Bellevalia trifoliata*)

Crown anemone (*Anemone coronaria*)

Iris (*Iris sisyrinchum*)

Winged pea (*Tetragonolobus purpureus*)

Carmine crowfoot (*Ranunculus asiaticus*)

Common corn flag (*Gladiolus segetum*)

Dyer's alkanet (*Alkanna lehmanii*)

Asphodel (*Asphodelus fistolosus*)

Everlasting sun-gold (*Helichrysum stoechas*)

Horned red poppy (*Glaucium corniculatum*)

Wood daisy (*Bellis sylvestris*)

Rock rose (*Cistus creticus*)

Yellow crowfoot (*Ranunculus asiaticus*)

Crown daisy
(*Chrysanthemum coronarium L.*)

Red and yellow crowfoot
(*Ranunculus asiaticus*)

Yellow rock rose
(*Helianthemum H. obtusifolium*)

Buffavento Castle

Least well-preserved and most inaccessible of the three castles in the Girne (Kyrenia) Range, Buffavento Castle's origins are obscure. We know that it was standing in 1191, when Richard the Lionheart of England captured the island, since the chronicler Benedict of Peterborough records: '... thus was delivered to him (Richard) the exceeding strong castle of Buffevent, and after that all the towns and fortresses of the Empire were surrendered.' The name Buffavento, meaning 'buffeted by the wind', graphically describes its isolated position, from which one gains a fine view of the Troodos mountains to the south, and of the entire Girne (Kyrenia) Range. In clear conditions one can even see the Taurus Mountains of mainland Turkey from the peak.

When the Venetians took control of Cyprus, they had insufficient men to garrison Buffavento adequately, and so they slighted the fortress, removing its cannons, its armaments and most of its roofs. Hence its poor condition today.

Below: A pine tree on a cliff's edge in the Girne (Kyrenia) Range.

This aerial view looks towards St Hilarion across the Girne/Lefkoşa (Kyrenia/Nicosia) pass (the Boğaz). The pass was originally formed by severe earth movements during the geological past, and today offers a direct route for the main road from Girne (Kyrenia) to Lefkoşa (Nicosia). The highest peak is Trypa Vouno, at 3000 feet (935 metres) on the opposite side of the pass from St Hilarion.

Inset: A shepherd's hound in an olive grove on the foothills of the Girne (Kyrenia) Range.

St Hilarion Castle

Westernmost of the three castles in the Girne (Kyrenia) Range, St Hilarion stands about four miles (six kilometres) from Girne (Kyrenia), and at a height of 2200 feet (660 metres). The castle apparently derives its name from a hermit named Hilarion, who fled the Holy Land following the Arab invasion. The present castle was built by the Byzantines, and was surrendered by Isaac Comnenus to Richard the Lionheart and Guy de Lusignan in 1191. Under the Lusignans, the castle's defences were greatly strengthened, while during the thirteenth century the stronghold also became a summer residence for the royal family.

Inset: The Middle Ward, St Hilarion Castle.

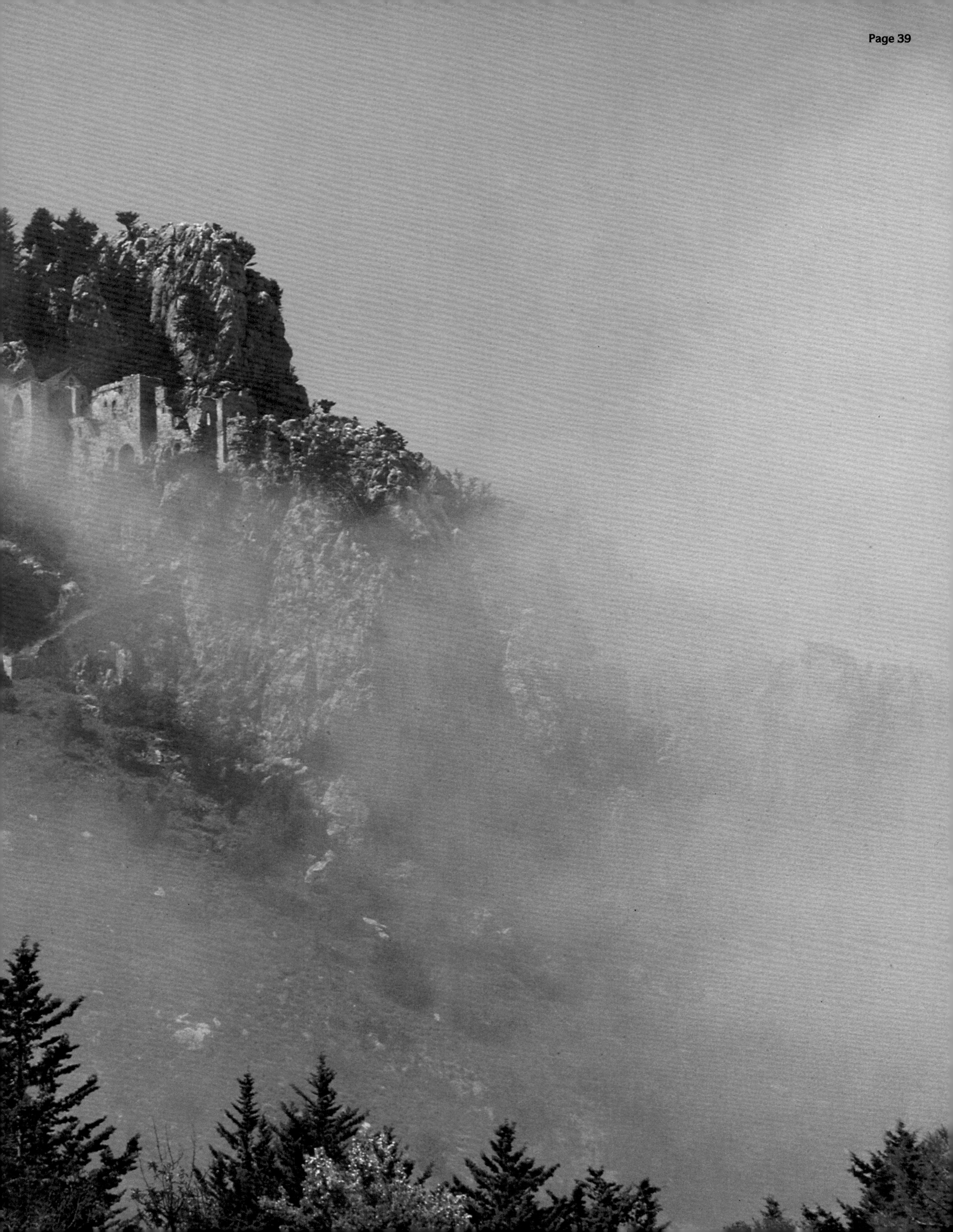

St Hilarion Castle

After the Venetians occupied Cyprus in 1489, they dismantled St Hilarion Castle to save the expense of garrisoning it and because its defences had been rendered ineffective with the invention of gunpowder. However, the main sections of the castle as they were under the Lusignans can still be distinguished: a lower ward, on the south slopes beneath the rocky summit; a middle ward, on the eastern shoulder; and an upper ward, between the twin peaks of the summit (in the Middle Ages the castle was sometimes known as Didymus – 'the twins'). The Lusignan royal apartments are situated in the upper ward. In the aerial picture, the town of Girne (Kyrenia) can be seen in the distance.

Inset: A vaulted passageway in the gatehouse, St Hilarion Castle.

Jousting Ground, St Hilarion Castle

Below the lower ward of the castle lies the medieval jousting ground, where knights would exercise and practise tilting on horseback. The level area of the jousting ground is clearly visible in the foreground of the aerial picture, while the Mediterranean coast and the town of Girne (Kyrenia) are beyond.

Below: Karaman (Karmi), a little village situated high in the hills west of Girne (Kyrenia), just below St Hilarion Castle. The village boasts a typical village church, with white-washed walls and a little belfry; the road from Karaman (Karmi) offers magnificent views over the Mediterranean.

Girne (Kyrenia) Range

The Girne (Kyrenia) Range, viewed from the Mediterranean Sea to the north. The long north coast of Cyprus has always been perilous to mariners battling against the prevailing north-west or north-east winds, and the little horse-shoe shaped harbour of Girne (Kyrenia) offered one of the few safe havens. This view is taken from east of the town of Girne (Kyrenia).

Inset: Olive grove and young wheat on the coastal plain, northern coast of Kıbrıs.

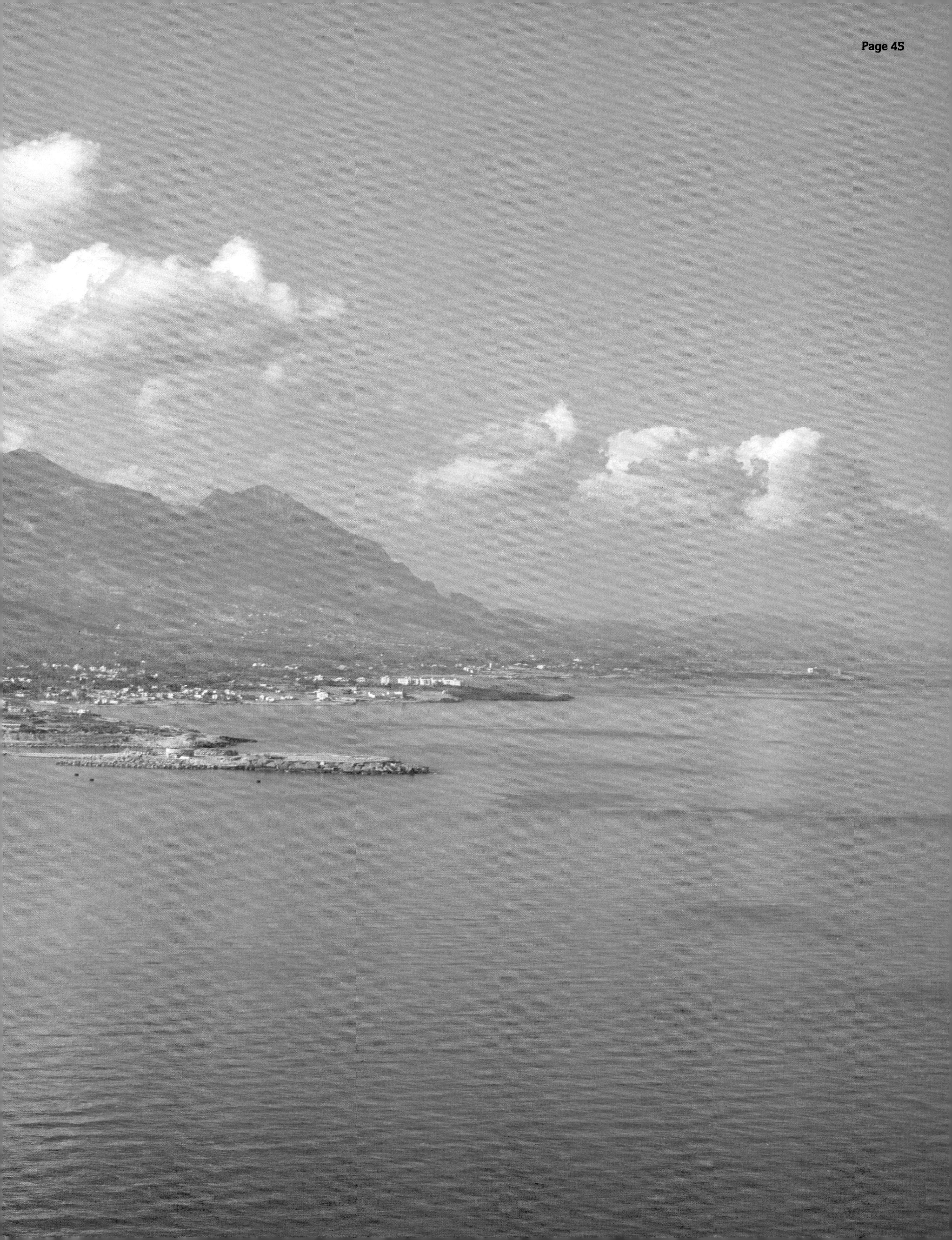

Girne (Kyrenia)

The origins of Girne (Kyrenia) are obscure; it has been claimed that King Cyrus of Persia founded the town when he captured Cyprus. Kyrenia was at one time one of the nine kingdoms of Cyprus. A little Byzantine chapel, now within the ramparts of Girne (Kyrenia) Castle, dates from at least as early as the ninth century A.D., but most of the fortification was carried out by the Lusignans and Venetians. The town was completely walled in during the Middle Ages, but most of those walls have now disappeared, though three of the medieval towers (or bastions) are still standing.

The modern town of Girne (Kyrenia) has spread well outside the medieval limits; it reaches south towards the mountains, and both east and west along the coast, where clean, sandy beaches offer ideal locations for villas and hotels. The aerial picture shows part of the old town, clustered around the harbour. The minaret of the Aga Cafer Paşa Mosque, built about 1580 by Aga Cafer Paşa, is in the centre of the picture.

Below: The harbour, Girne (Kyrenia). The ferry boat to Anamur, on the Turkish coast, is moored to the jetty.

Girne (Kyrenia) Harbour

During the Middle Ages, the merchants of Venice made Girne (Kyrenia) an important trading post, safeguarding the trade routes from India and China to the West. However, with the discovery of the sea route to the East via the Cape in the sixteenth century, trade decreased rapidly in the eastern Mediterranean. Girne (Kyrenia) declined in importance, although a trickle of trade continued, including such merchandise as jewellery, spices, timber, dyes, wool and silk. With the opening of the Suez Canal in the late nineteenth century, ports in the eastern Mediterranean once more rose in importance. A new jetty was built at Girne (Kyrenia), and the port thoroughly dredged to allow entry to larger vessels.

Below: The splendidly sited Dome Hotel, Girne (Kyrenia), near the harbour.

Girne (Kyrenia) Castle

The first buildings on this site probably date back as far as Hellenistic and Roman times, although the origins of the present castle probably date only to the seventh century A.D., when the Byzantines wanted to defend Girne (Kyrenia) against Arab raiders. Much of the present castle was constructed by King John Dibelin between 1208–1211, and the Lusignans resided here during both war and peace. Girne (Kyrenia) Castle was badly damaged by the Venetians during their raids in 1373, and then captured by them in 1491.

During the Venetian occupation of Cyprus, the defences of Girne (Kyrenia) Castle were altered to take account of the new age of gunpowder, with lower walls and rounded towers. Inside the castle today stands the Church of St George, dating from the early Byzantine period, when it stood *outside*. The tomb of the Turkish admiral Sadık Paşa, who captured Girne (Kyrenia) in 1570, is found in the entrance to the castle.

Below: A merchant ship dating from *c.* 300 B.C., raised from the sea bed of the Mediterranean near Girne (Kyrenia) and preserved in the Shipwreck Museum, Girne (Kyrenia) Castle. Recovered by marine archaeologists between 1967–69, the ship is probably the earliest trading vessel yet discovered. The museum also contains the original cargo and equipment from the ancient ship.

Deniz Kızı Bay

Deniz Kızı, 'mermaid beach', is one of the finest and most popular beaches on the entire north coast of Cyprus. Only a few miles west of Girne (Kyrenia), it is remarkable for its green foliage in high summer. Some hundred acacia trees surround the splendidly situated Deniz Kızı Hotel (aerial photograph), and in spring there is a feast of colourful flowers. The beach is contained within an idyllic bay, enclosed by a rocky promontory on each side.

Below: Two Cyprus pottery exhibits from the display in the Deniz Kızı Hotel. Left: An oil flask dating from the eighth century B.C., and turned on a potter's wheel; right: a smaller flask, dating from the Middle Bronze Age (c. seventeenth century B.C.) made without the use of a potter's wheel.

Bellapais Abbey

Bellapais Abbey, the most impressive Gothic building in Cyprus, is situated on a natural terrace overlooking the village of Ozanköy (Kazaphani). Originally founded in the twelfth century by monks of the Augustinian order, by 1206 it had been taken over by the Premonstratensian order. The Lusignan King Hugh III (1267–1284) was the abbey's principal benefactor, probably largely responsible for the building whose remains we see today. King Hugh died at Tyre, on the Mediterranean coast of Palestine, but his body was brought back to Cyprus and he was buried at Bellapais.

By 1540 the lives of the monks of Bellapais had become degenerate and rumours were circulating of polygamous practices at the abbey. As a result by 1570 Bellapais had been deserted and was already beginning to run to ruin.

Below: The ruins of Bellapais Abbey. The prominent cypress trees were planted by a recent custodian of the abbey.

Mesarya (Mesaoria) Plain

South of the Girne (Kyrenia) Range, and stretching south-west towards the great central massif of Troodos, lies the Mesarya (Mesaoria) or Central Plain. In pre-historical times, this plain lay beneath the sea, which separated the two mountain ranges. Although this plain was at one time thickly covered with woodlands, most of the trees were cut down in historical times to provide timber for Egypt. Today the area around Lefkoşa (Nicosia) provides staple crops for the island. The eastern end of the Girne (Kyrenia) Range can be seen in the distance.

Inset: Sheep at sunset, in the plains south of the Girne (Kyrenia) Range.

Güzelyurt (Morphou) Plain

The plains around Güzelyurt (Morphou) are very fertile, supporting rich crops of citrus fruit in extensive orchards. The oranges, lemons and grapefruit provide one of the island's principal exports. The aerial picture shows some of the carefully-spaced plantations of citrus trees near Güzelyurt (Morphou). The town of Güzelyurt (Morphou) is an important market and business centre. It was formerly the centre of a thriving copper mining industry, dating back to the Bronze Age. Modern Güzelyurt (Morphou) has some fascinating craft-shops and an interesting museum.

Inset: Orange trees near Güzelyurt (Morphou).

Vuni (Vouni) Palace

Vuni (Vouni) Palace, situated about forty miles (sixty-five kilometres) west of Lefkoşa (Nicosia), on the highest peak in the area, apparently dates from the fifth century B.C.. The site was excavated by the Swedish Cyprus archaeological expedition in 1928–9, and it is thought the palace was built by the Persians in an attempt to overawe the rebellious citizens of nearby Soli.

In 449 B.C. the Athenian general Kimon established a new pro-Greek dynasty on Cyprus, and Vuni (Vouni) was probably taken over by the new rulers at this time; certainly Hellenistic features have been found dating from this period. However, *c.* 380 B.C. the inhabitants of Soli succeeded in destroying the palace of Vuni (Vouni), originally built with the intention of overawing them.

Below: View north towards the sea from Vuni (Vouni).

Vuni (Vouni) **Palace**

The palace and its surrounding buildings were encircled by a rampart wall, and the area inside the wall divided into three main terraces. The topmost of these terraces was occupied by a small temple of the goddess Athena; the second, and largest, by the palace and its surrounding sanctuaries and temples; and the third, below the palace, by a residential area stretching towards the sea. The three terraces are linked by a series of narrow roads and steps. The state apartments of the palace of Vuni (Vouni) are similar in their arrangement to the Mycenaean palaces.

Below: The Service Court, Vuni (Vouni) Palace. A bottle-shaped cistern was cut into the rock at the seaward end of the courtyard to collect rainwater from the roofs of the storerooms.

INDEX

Acknowledgements

We wish to express our most sincere thanks to His Excellency President Rauf Denktaş for making it possible for us to carry out this project; we hope we have made a contribution towards promoting tourism to Kıbrıs (Northern Cyprus). We also want to thank Mary Gibson for first introducing us to Hilmi Özen, Director of the National Theatre of Kıbrıs (Northern Cyprus), who worked so hard, first arranging our flight, and then spending many hours gathering together the details and facts needed for the text. We must also thank our two pilots, Colonels Arı and Altın, for their professional skill and patience. We are grateful to Darren Hedges of Protocol Colour Laboratory for his expert work, and also wish to thank Harry Lewis of Pentax (U.K.) Ltd., and C.T.A., London. We are grateful to the Director of the Archaeological Museum for verifying the manuscript. Without the unstinting help of all our friends in Northern Cyprus, and of our personal assistants, Diana Irons and Shelagh Rump, this book simply would not have been possible.

Sonia Halliday and Laura Lushington, May 1987